I0144099

"Every person over 75 has two missions in life:
1. to remain independent and in control
2. to be remembered"

I heard the above at a National Academy of Elder Law Attorneys conference years ago. It struck me how fundamental and true it is. Considering these two needs, we can easily grasp the threat that long term care is for elders, indeed, for all of us. It threatens complete loss. Loss of control, loss of home and l savings to the nursing home, loss of all quality of life.

An elder needs to remain in control and have his or her wishes complied with. That is what powers of attorneys or trusts do: they give an elder the ability to name whom she trusts to do what needs to be done. She can "fire" them if they do not do what she wants. But is more

But, there is more to . It is about how to remain independent, and how to maximize the quality of life.

On the second point: What is a Will about? It is about being remembered. The desire to provide for one's family after death is a fundamental human need and should never be underestimated.

I have made this my life's work. My mission is to help you or your parents, or whomever you are caring for accomplish your life's mission. Long term care requires planning and strong, *informed*, action. By this booklet I try to complete my mission. I must motivate you to take action now, or I have failed. I hope you will understand if I prod you to action now and again.

Thanks and All the Best to you.

Jim Schuster,
Certified Elder Law Attorney
Of Counsel to Cummings, McClorey Davis & Acho
Livonia, Michigan

"I need someone to give me a hand here."

There are two reasons elders want help: convenience and incapacity. By convenience I mean assistance makes it easier to deal with the "modern world." A senior who is hard of hearing may not be able to use the phone to take care of medical appointments and other business. An elder experiencing cognitive decline may be able to handle daily matters but cannot handle more complex matters. These sorts of disabilities are to be expected with aging and should be contemplated and planned for.

"Incapacity"

A person is *legally* incapacitated when he or she cannot make necessary decisions of financial, medical or legal matters. The incapacity may be temporary or long term, total or partial. Under the law, capacity is not determined by a medical diagnosis, though such diagnosis may explain the loss of capacity. Legal capacity to perform a legal act varies with the matter at hand. A person recently diagnosed Alzheimer's dementia may have the ability to decide who he trusts to handle financial and medical decisions. However, he may lack the capacity to make a financial investment or understand a multi-page contract. He will need somebody to do those things for him.

The failure to prepare in advance for incapacity: Probate

A legal ruling of incapacity may only be made by a court after a public hearing. If an elder makes no preparation in advance for the time when she cannot manage her daily affairs, then the probate court may be the only option. If she has capacity she could execute a "power of attorney" and name an "agent" to manage things. If she is incapacitated without the ability to make a legal decision then the only option is petition to the probate court for the appointment of a guardian or conservator. We will call it "Lifetime Probate" to distinguish from probate of property after death or "Decedent's Probate"

One of the saddest cases I had was that of John. He was an independent lifetime bachelor who had saved over a million dollars during a lifetime as a toolmaker. He was in his mid-eighties when he developed cognitive impairment. He ended up with an attorney appointed his guardian and conservator who put him in a locked assisted living facility. His nephew had to come from Colorado to hire an attorney just to go to probate court and have an investigation and hearing so that John could be returned to his home with help by a home care agency. However, the probate court allowed the attorney to remain in control of his savings. After he died all his property went through probate. We never did find out how much those attorney fees were. All of this was completely avoidable. We will show you how in the pages that follow. Please heed the lesson from John's experience.

NOTES

DO NO PLANNING IN ADVANCE = LIFETIME PROBATE
The legally incapacitated individual

Lifetime probate means loss of control. The probate court appoints a person who will manage all the elder's affairs. The elder will likely be under court supervision for the rest of his or her life.

Probate Court proceeding. Requires:

+ Petition alleging facts supporting incapacity, which means the person is without the ability to care for himself.
+ Guardian Ad Litem. The court will appoint an attorney to make an investigation and report to the court.
+ Public hearing, not private, in "open court." The evidence presented must detail and prove incapacity.

Guardian

- Makes personal decisions for the Incapacitated Person, such as where to live, what medical treatment to be had.
- Must file an annual report
- Compensation and Expenses are allowed upon court approval

Conservator

- Manages the money and property of the Incapacitated Person
- Must file an Inventory
- Must file an Annual Account detailing all income and expenditures
- Compensation and Expenses are allowed upon court approval

Probate Pro

- Safe way to provide for persons who cannot help themselves
- The only alternative if no trustworthy person to serve as agent
- Provides oversight of those managing an elder's personal and financial affairs
- Provides a forum for resolving disputes
- Decisions are made in public court after all evidence is provided
- Authority of Guardian/Conservator almost never questioned
- Authority can be enforced by Probate Court

Probate Con

- Expensive - court fees, attorney fees, bond and conservator fees
- Slow, cumbersome process, can take months to get a decision
- Public proceedings expose embarrassing private information.
- May not be changed without court approval, hearing will be required

NOTES

HOW TO EMPOWER YOUR ADVOCATE

Life Care Planning

If the Elder has the mental capacity to authorize a trusted person to make medical, legal and financial decisions then he or she can execute documents that empower an "agent" to handle matters. These may encompass all of daily living from paying bills to arranging and managing medical care. The agent must be informed and empowered to address matters of a complete change in daily living, such as selling the family home and moving into an assisted living facility, getting quality medical care. Life Care planning contemplates the best quality of life with dignity and self-direction.

Few would disagree that handling medical matters is the most important job an agent can do. So we start with what may be the most important legal document.

1. Medical/Healthcare Power of Attorney (MPOA)

This legal document *may save your life*. If an agent is appointed to handle the entire range of medical matters then you can be best assured that you will get the care you need, not the care that is the cheapest. The necessary components are:

- The MPOA must be immediately effective so agent can deal with emergencies and routine medical matters without obtaining a doctor's letter of incapacity.
- **HIPAA.** The agent must be authorized to receive confidential medical information
- **Designation of Patient Advocate.** Under Michigan law a patient can execute a "Designation of Patient Advocate" who will then be empowered to make End of Life Treatment decisions if the patient is unable to participate in informed medical decision making. Two doctors must make the determination of inability to participate. This document takes place of the 'living will.'
- **General Healthcare Power.** The agent must be to handle daily medical matters e.g. doctors' appointments, insurance questions, prescription questions even though the patient may be able to do it herself
- **Mental Health Code.** The agent must be given specific authority to make decisions regarding mental health matters such as treatment for depression, anxiety, aggressive or physically defensive behavior, or "agitation."

Recommendation:

Everybody *must* have a complete healthcare power of attorney. Your advocate cannot help you unless you have given an *immediately effective* healthcare power of attorney with full authority under HIPAA, the Michigan Public Health Code and Mental Health Code.

NOTES

THE ADVANCE DIRECTIVE ("LIVING WILL")

Perhaps the most difficult decision for the patient advocate is when to terminate medical treatment of a terminally ill patient. Sometimes the decision is clearly supported by medical advice and the facts of the situation. Sometimes it comes as a surprise as when a patient has a rare complication from surgery.

A person has the constitutional right to accept or reject medical treatment. It continues even if the patient cannot communicate, then the "patient advocate" may make the decision according to the patient's instructions. The advocate must be duly authorized under law before making the decision.

LAW
DNR:, "Michigan Do-not-resuscitate Procedure Act MCL 333.1051.
1. If the patient has no vital signs, no pulse or not breathing, and if he or she completed a DNR health professional shall not attempt to resuscitate the declarant.
2. The DNR must be signed by the declarant or the patient advocate and the patient's physician.

Designation of Patient Advocate Act MCL 700.5506
1. A person may appoint a patient advocate who can make end of life medical decisions that may allow the patient to die.
2. The patient advocate designation must be executed in the presence of and signed by 2 witnesses who may not be the named patient advocate, patient's spouse, parent, child, grandchild, sibling, presumptive heir, known devisee at the time of the witnessing, physician, or an employee of a medical provider for the patient, or of a home for the aged where the patient lives.
3. The advocate may authorize the termination of treatment when it is clear that the patient would have refused the treatment under the circumstances
4. A patient advocate may make a decision to withhold or withdraw treatment that would allow a patient to die only if the patient has expressed in a clear and convincing manner that the patient advocate is authorized to make such a decision, and that such a decision could or would allow the patient's death.
5. The authority under a patient advocate designation is exercisable by a patient advocate only when the patient is unable to participate in medical treatment decisions. The patient's attending physician and another physician or licensed psychologist shall determine upon examination of the patient when the patient is unable to participate in medical treatment decisions.

NOTES

GENERAL DURABLE POWER OF ATTORNEY

A general durable power of attorney (DPOA) is not limited to specific matters such as medical, finances or real estate. Its purpose is to authorize the agent to handle all the elder's matters. The term "durable" means it is still effective even after the "principal" is incapacitated. While it is possible to have a durable power of attorney that is limited it is better if it is general so that your agent can handle any matter that needs attention.

- **Specific Authority.** An agent, sometimes called "attorney in fact" can only handle matters that are expressly authorized, nothing else.
- A DPOA *requires* reliable and trustworthy person to serve as Agent

A DPOA should grant complete powers concerning all business elder has including:
- Pension Plans, IRAs
- Real Estate, investments, Stocks/Mutual Funds
- Annuities, Insurance
- Government Benefits
- Trusts
- Credit Cards
- Applying for government benefits and the accompanying gifting and asset transferring powers. The agent will also need the power to "self-deal."
- Must consider whether to authorize pre-dispute compulsory arbitration (giving up the right to go to court)
- **Extraordinary powers** - self dealing, gifting, employing and compensating family members, establishing a trust and so on are needed for "Asset Protection" and must be expressly given.

Pro
- Inexpensive
- Elder remains in control, grants permission to another to act
- May be changed or revoked at any time

Con
- If elder is incapacitated, is unable to supervise
- Can be tool of elder abuser
- Service is voluntary; Agent is not required to act
- Can be rejected by providers, especially "Wall Street" investment companies

Recommendation: Everybody *must* have a general power of attorney. Without it you cannot take care of all business of another person including your spouse. Your alternative is lifetime probate.

NOTES

PATIENT ADVOCACY: A NECESSITY

Getting good healthcare can be a life or death matter. If a person cannot manage her own care, a patient advocate is mandatory. Healthcare is not an informal and friendly as it may have been in the mythical days of Dr. Marcus Welby. Medicine has gotten extremely complicated. Your doctor does not do it all anymore. There are treatments that only specialists can administer and oversee. When you go to the hospital, you will have an "attending physician" or "hospitalist" who will coordinate with the specialists of the treatment team. Your doctor will not visit. Your advocate will need to have HIPAA authority to ask questions and discuss treatment with your doctors.

First Rule of Advocacy
Ask questions. Be clear on the treatment plan. Know the medications, their side-effects and their contraindications.

Two Most Common Causes of Malpractice Complaints
1) Failure of doctor to check new medications against ones the patient is currently taking for side effects and contraindications.
2) Failure to follow up on lab tests and act on any abnormalities found.

Medicare Issues in the Hospital and Post-hospital Setting.
- The fundamental right of Medicare beneficiaries is medical treatment that is "necessary and reasonable."
- Observation Status: You must know whether a patient is "admitted" to the hospital or is on "observation status." The first is covered by Medicare A and the second is by Medicare B. If the patient is not admitted there could be a large bill not covered by Medicare. You can speak to your doctors about changing your status to being "admitted." They will need to review the treatment you received to see if that can be done.
- Discharge Plan: A medical provider must make a discharge plan upon termination of hospital or skilled care nursing facility care. These plans must be designed to enable patients to achieve their highest practicable level of functioning.
- Premature Termination of Skilled Care: A court case called Jimmo restated a patient's right to necessary skilled medical care to be paid for by Medicare. This includes post hospital "rehab" both in rehab center and at home. It should not be terminated merely because a patient stopped "making progress." It should be continued if merely to maintain function, which would be lost without the care.
- Appeals: If you are denied treatment that is "necessary and reasonable," then get your doctor's support and appeal Do learn the process of your particular benefit whether it concerns traditional Medicare, Medicare Advantage or Medicare D your prescription plan.

NOTES

NURSING HOME ADVOCACY

The resident in a nursing home has rights guaranteed by law. Since residents are often too sick to manage their care, these rights may only be effected by an informed patient and authorized advocate.

Resident's Rights: The patient/resident has the right to:
1. Achieve and Maintain the Highest Practicable Level of Functioning
2. Make Health Care Decisions
3. Accommodation of Individual Needs and Preferences
4. Be Free of Unnecessary Restraints
5. Be Free From physical or mental abuse
6. Have her own doctor and have treatment plan of nursing home reviewed.

In practical terms these rights mean that the patient has the right to an individualized care plan. Too often facility doctors terminate a resident's medical treatment plan in favor of one that makes it easier to manage the resident. The advocate must be alert for any decline in the patient's health or functioning. The advocate may insist that the resident's personal physician determine the care plan.

Long Term Care Ombudsman (LTCO). The patient advocate should know who is assigned to the nursing home from the LTCO. The advocate will need their help in case of a dispute over care of the resident. Their number is (866) 485-9393.

Be on the Lookout for: sudden weight loss; sudden loss of ability to communicate or relate to visitors; lethargy; unexplained change in medication. Be present for bathing and be alert for development of bed sores. Mark bandages so you know if they are changed.
• Learn about dangers of antibiotics with an elderly patient and learn the warning signs.
• Learn about the dangers of mood medications (psychotropic) that are often prescribed with a resident is "agitated."
• Learn about the dangers of dehydration and changes in electrolyte levels
• Know the warning signs of deadly reaction to medications
• Weight loss is a sign of declining health, find out what is going on.
• Be on the lookout for decubitus ulcers (bedsores) and monitor treatment.

NOTES

CAREGIVERS

When a child is an elderly parent's caregiver she, or he, is often the "care manager," the "financial manager" the "healthcare manager" and to coin a term the overall "Life Manager." Whatever the elder needs the caregiver takes care of it. Many avoidable legal problems can grow out of the elder-caregiver relationship.

Legal Issue, Compensation:

- Under the general law the value of child caregiver services is $0.00. The legal presumption is that the child performs the service for "love and affection." It does not matter if she or he suffers loss of health or financial means. Some siblings have the same view.
- If the elder pays any caregiver, family or not, the elder is an "employer" must pay the employer's taxes and is subject to workers compensation and unemployment insurance laws. The caregiver is an "employee" subject to income tax withholding and payment of Social Security and Medicare Tax. However, if you use an agency then they are the employer.

Elder Abuse:

- Often a Caregiver is a person of "trust and confidence" and is under increased scrutiny for elder abuse. Complete records of all financial transactions must be kept. In addition the Caregiver will be held responsible for the elder's for harm to the elder's physical and emotional health.

Potential Problems: Caregiver Child and Siblings

If siblings feel forced out of parent's life they may battle in probate court for control of parent, for control of money or make charges of physical, emotional of financial elder abuse.

Caregiver Contract

- The caregiver contract is a solution to the problems presented. An agreement is made at onset with all family involved. What authority shall be given? Who will handle financial, legal and medical matters? Should the Caregiver be compensated or not? Are Medicaid or Veterans benefits contemplated?
- All terms are agreed to including who has what responsibilities and authority. If compensation is to be made a contract will be drawn up stating the services, frequency and compensation. comply with tax and employment laws. Medical proof of need for the services will be obtained. The proof will satisfy VA and Medicaid requirements. The Fair Market Value of the services will be determined.

NOTES

ASSET PROTECTION

What does "asset protection" mean?

It means that you are protecting your property from some threat. We buy homeowner's insurance to protect our home from fire, and life insurance to provide a way to take care of our family after we die. Billionaires use asset protection strategies to minimize taxes and to minimize law suits.

In the elder law context the term is mostly used to save our property for our spouse and family from the bankrupting cost of long term care in a nursing home.

Irrevocable Grantor Trust

While there are a number of asset protection *strategies* the number one *legal document* for asset protection is the irrevocable trust. Specialized irrevocable trusts are used for asset protection in case of: lawsuits; Veterans Pension benefits; and Medicaid asset protection. These trusts may allow you to receive the income but not principal from the trust. Once your property is in an irrevocable trust, you cannot take it back. If the trust is not properly administered it could fail.

For example, suppose you applied for Medicaid and you had $400,000 in the trust. Suppose the Inspector General investigated and found that your trustee distributed $75,000 to your children who then "loaned it to you" in the five years before you applied. Medicaid would be denied and your trustee could be in court fighting the Attorney General. Attorney fees could be in the tens of thousands of dollars.

These trusts are for people who have a substantial amount of money they do not intend to spend. Here are some points to consider.

- Are you likely to get sued? Do you have sufficient insurance?
- What are you preserving assets <u>for</u>? What are you protecting <u>against</u>?
- Would it be okay for you go to a nursing home, while the trust has significant assets in it, instead of you receiving care in your home?
- Will you be able to afford nursing home alternatives that Medicaid does not pay for such as assisted living facilities (that might cost $6,000+ per month)?
- Can you accomplish your goals without the cost of the trust and the annual maintenance?

Recommendation: Consult with an experienced elder law attorney before you execute an asset protection plan, be that making gifts to children, executing an irrevocable trust or purchasing an annuity. If a proposed plan of action does not feel right there is always another way to do it. Get a second opinion.

NOTES

GOVERNMENT BENEFITS -- VETERANS ADMINISTRATION

The following programs are administered by the VA, "Veterans Administration."

Disability Compensation

VA Compensation benefits are for those veterans injured during service. The amount of the cash benefit is determined by the percentage rating. (See below)

• Disability must be service connected, can be aggravation of existing condition.

• Vietnam Veterans who served "in country" are presumed eligible if they have prostate or respiratory cancer; ischemic heart disease; Parkinson's disease, and some other conditions. See the VA for more information.

• Veterans Stationed at Camp Lejune 30 days or more during 1950s - 1980s and have a presumed condition such as a cancer are eligible. See VA for more information.

• A Claim can be made years after service, such as hearing loss of WWII Vet.

• Rating may be increased if condition worsens over years.

• May receive additional Special Monthly Compensation if housebound or require the aid and attendance of someone to perform daily living functions.

• Benefits are non-taxable and are not based on income or net worth.

Compensation Rate Table - 2018

Rating %	10	20	30	40	50
Veteran Alone	$136.24	$269.30	$417.15	$600.90	$855.41
Veteran with Spouse	"	"	$466.15	$666.90	$937.41
Rating %	60	70	80	90	100
Veteran Alone	$1,083.52	$1,365.48	$1,587.25	$1,783.68	$2,973.86
Veteran with Spouse	$1,182.52	$1,481.48	$1,719.25	$1,932.68	$3,139.67

Special Improved Pension

Homebound and Aid and Attendance Rated

• Wartime Veterans: Service must be between the dates

World War II	12/07/1941 – 12/31/1946
Korea	06/25/1950 – 01/31/1955
Vietnam (in-country only)	02/28/1961 – 08/04/1964
Vietnam	08/05/1964 – 05/07/1975

NOTES

VA Pension Benefit points to remember:

- "Disabled." Age 65 and up qualifies as being disabled.
  Provides cash, tax free, support for "Unreimbursed Medical Expense" (UME)
- UME not only includes uncovered medical or pharmacy bills, but also includes paid help that an aide provides with personal needs such as bathing and other "ADLs" (Activities of Daily Living). Payment to family members for assistance qualifies as UME.
- UME includes the cost of necessary residential care for a Vet with a cognitive condition such as dementia. If the Vet needs a safe living residence such as a "Memory care unit" in "assisted living" facility, the expense is UME.
- Maximum benefit when UME is equal or greater than monthly income.
- Asset ("net worth") limited program. Net worth may be reduced by transferring assets.
- No "look back" on property or "asset" transfers made to reduce net worth.
- VA benefit planning may conflict with Medicaid, which states if divestment occurs within 5 years of application a "penalty period" will be imposed. During this time Medicaid will not pay nursing home or MiChoice waiver benefits. The period can be avoided if all assets are returned prior to application.
- An annuity used to reduce net worth for VA benefit is Medicaid divestment.
- An annuity used to supplement VA benefits will end up going to nursing home or government Medicaid Estate Recovery upon death.

Definitions:

"Service Pension" or "surviving spouse pension" for those age 65 or older or totally and permanently disabled, whose income and net worth is not sufficient to live off for a reasonable period of time.

"Housebound" means substantially confined to his or her home because of a permanent disability.

"Aid and Attendance" means require the aid of another person in order to perform activities of daily living, such as bathing, feeding, dressing, toileting, adjusting prosthetic devices, or protecting yourself from the hazards of your daily environment or is legally blind.

Veteran Pension -- Maximum Annual Pension Rate (2018)

Status	Annual	Monthly
Service Pension - Veteran	$13,166	$1097
Veteran + 1 Dependent	$17,241	$1437
Housebound Veteran	$16,089	$1341
Housebound Veteran + 1	$20,166	$1681
Aid & Attendance Veteran	$21,962	$1830
Aid & Attendance Veteran + 1	$26,036	$2170

NOTES

Surviving Spouse "Death Pension" Maximum Payment (2018)

Status	Annual	Monthly
Surviving Spouse	$8,830	$736
Housebound Surviving Spouse	$10,792	$899
Aid & Attendance Surviving	$14,113	$1176

Refund to VA

The Pension benefit is calculated on an *annual basis,* that is benefits are awarded per *benefit year.* At the end of the year, expect the VA to review the recipients received income and UME. If income was more or UME less than the amount expected, *the VA may seek refund.* The VA will also review the recipient's reported income, and use tax records to review. If income during the year, including one time payments, is greater than calculated the VA may demand refund.

VA Health Care Benefits

The veteran must be enrolled in VA Healthcare (VHA) to receive benefits. The following are just some of the benefits of VHA. Benefits are subject to physician order and implementation by hospital social worker. Not all benefits are available in all areas. Contact your VA hospital/facility to learn about program availability.

Community Adult Day Care

Benefit provides social interaction for vets who need assistance with activities of daily living.

Home Health Aide

Provides medically necessary services including assistance with ADLs and household tasks to maintain safe living for veteran. Program may be used for respite for vet's caregiver. VA uses private contractors to provide from 2 to 42 hours per week.

Veteran Directed Care

This benefit provides cash payment for non-agency aides to Veterans at risk of nursing home placement. Vet hires aides, may be friends or family, to provide home care services so the vet can live independently in-home. It is not available in all areas.

NOTES

GOVERNMENT BENEFITS -- MEDICAID

Means Tested
Medicaid is "means tested" which means the applicant must meet asset and income limits. Michigan has two long term care programs. The MiChoice Waiver provides long term care services in the person's residence. It has asset and income caps. The nursing home program has the same asset limits but no income limit as long as the person's income is less than the cost of the nursing home.

Medicaid In-Home -- "MiChoice" Medicaid Waiver
This program is administered the Area Agencies on Aging and a few other agencies. The goal of the Medicaid Waiver program is to enable recipients to live in their own residence and minimize institutional care. However the program has limited openings, "slots", and these are allocated according to service priority. The two highest are those who are in a nursing home, the nursing facility transition initiative (NFTI) and those whose medical condition puts them at "imminent risk" for nursing home placement. Applicants with lesser needs may have significant waiting periods.
- "Medicaid Waiver" has all asset rules of Nursing Home Medicaid
- Is income capped. If income is more than $2,250 may not receive benefit
- Program provides services such as personal care, home delivered meals, private duty nursing, housekeeping and transportation.
- Program will not provide total support or 24 hour care
- May be coordinated with and supplement VA benefits
- It is subject to after death "Medicaid Estate Recovery" (can be avoided)

Medicaid - Nursing Home
- "Spend Down" to $2,000 of "countable assets"
- Applicant must be in a nursing home "Medicaid Bed"
- Applicant and spouse allowed "exempt assets" e.g. home, car, funeral plan
- At home spouse is allowed to keep half of "countable assets" to a maximum of $123,600. Any more than that must be either be spent down or "sheltered."
- Assets of married and single applicants can be "sheltered" ("asset protection")
- 5 year "look back" on "divestment" (gifts and other transfers)
- After death "Medicaid Estate Recovery" against the home

Excluded Assets and Countable Assets
Assets of applicants are sorted into two categories. Excluded assets include a home, personal possessions, vehicle and funeral plan. Countable assets include everything else that could be reduced to cash. Countable assets must be spent down.

NOTES

Medicaid "Spend Down"

In 2018 single Medicaid applicants must "spend down" their "countable assets" to $2,000. Married couples may save up to $123,600 more of countable assets for the "Community Spouse Resource Allowance. Applicants may spend on anything for themselves, their spouse or their property. They may purchase new items, fix or repair current property.

Medicaid Estate Recovery

Long term care Medicaid comes with "estate recovery" which means the recipient must pay back the government the amount of benefits paid out. It does not matter whether the recipient paid a lifetime of social security and income taxes. The pay back is collected out of the deceased recipient's probate estate. If probate is avoided the government recovers nothing.

A "Lady Bird" deed avoids probate and Medicaid Estate Recovery, under the current law.

Recommendation

If you are trying to save your home and life-savings (assets) see an experienced elder law attorney. The Medicaid programs are complicated and contrary. There is misinformation everywhere. Do the smart thing. After all, everybody gets help with taxes and these programs are much more complicated.

NOTES

ESTATE PLANNING
Avoiding probate on death and directing who will get your property.

Estate planning means who gets what after I die and what conditions I want to put on my gift. It is also known as planning for "Death and Taxes." Note that only those with over $5 Million need to worry about *inheritance* taxes. Persons with large IRAs and 401k plans need to consider estate planning *income* taxes.

Joint Property - A Solution or a Problem?

Owning property jointly with a person who is not your spouse avoids probate on death. It does not a complete solution as it does not avoid lifetime probate. and it places your property at risk.

Joint Property Problems:
- Bankruptcy of Co-Owner - your joint property will be part of the bankrupt estate.
- Debt of Co-Owner - your property may be taken to pay the debt.
- "Borrowing" by Co-Owner - money may taken without your permission
- Financial Elder Abuse - same as "borrowing"
- Equity Co-Owner Veto - the joint owner can refuse to sell or mortgage.

Joint Property: Problems on Death:
- A Will can be defeated by joint ownership of accounts or property.
- No guarantee your wishes will be followed, children may dispute shares of accounts. Should a caregiver keep an account if she was the joint owner?
- Does not provide for payment of bills and taxes.
- One child may not agree to share joint property according to your Will
- If two or more children inherit property, such as a home or cottage, they will end up in court if they do not agree how to handle it.

Recommendation: In general joint property is not the best way to avoid probate and it can lead to worse problems. A trust is regarded as the safest comprehensive way to avoid probate, both during lifetime and on death. A Trust can help you remain independent while you are alive by providing management of all your business including your care.

Due to cost of a trust, many folks will find it good enough to have a Will and set up beneficiaries on all accounts and property in a way that matches the Will. Use powers of attorney to manage your affairs when you cannot, including medical. Keep beneficiary information current. Consult with an elder law attorney for the safest way

"Lady Bird Deed"

This deed transfers property to "remainder" persons upon death. The remainder may be joint so that only those who survive inherit or it can be as "Tenants in Common." This deed makes no provision for contingencies. If a child predeceases should his spouse or children take his share? Or should it lapse? They may end up in court

NOTES

A COMPLETE ESTATE PLAN

Will or Trust? You should have one or the other, but since the trust requires maintenance and initial extra expense, which should you choose? If the only goal is to avoid probate upon death, then the costs of a correctly administered estate even out the overall costs. The major trust fees are up front whereas major fees under the Will occur at the end. Some people forget that a properly administered trust estate does entail costs. Trust administration covers the same steps as probate administration, with the exception of filing a petition with the court and paying an inventory fee.

Revocable Living Trust

A trust has a place in Life Care planning. It provides safe, secure management of property during the "grantor's" incapacity. It also avoids probate upon death of the grantor.

Pro

- Once property is in trust, it is simple to have the named successor trustee take over management.
- Trusts are especially respected by investment providers.
- Almost never questioned
- Trustee is required to act according to trust instructions and in the grantor's best interest.

Con

- Initial expense of the trust.
- Provisions can be so complicated that an attorney is needed to interpret.
- Trustee can only manage property transferred to the trust. Cannot manage other property.
- Trust cannot handle all matters, e.g. Medical decision making, (requires MPOA), IRAs and other tax deferred accounts.

Special Trusts

A "discretionary trust" or a "supplemental needs trust" is the best way to handle property for a disabled person: a spouse with Alzheimer's or other cognitive impairment; an SSI recipient; a child with tax or bankruptcy problems; a convict.

Recommendation: Not everybody "needs a trust." Those who should consider a trust are those who have significant savings or multiple properties; those who need to care for a spouse or disabled child after they die; and singles that have significant savings with no children to help them through long term care. Note, an IRA cannot be put in a trust, but after death distributions can be controlled by a properly drafted trust.

NOTES

PROBATE - DECEDENT'S ESTATES

Why do we have probate? We might boil it down to two reasons: 1) we need to know who is the legal owner of property after death; and, 2) debts of the deceased do not disappear on death. Creditors including the tax authorities can use the legal process to seize property to pay bills owed. Probate has one advantage of terminating the opportunity to make a claim four months after the process begins. Otherwise creditors could wait years before making claims and filing cases in court.

On a family level, probate is the process to be sure property is properly transferred to the heirs and all disputes resolved.

Testamentary Trusts

A will can have trusts for special case devisees such as a spouse with long term care needs, a disabled child, a child who is in prison or has bankruptcy or IRS Problems.

The Probate Process

How slow is probate? The minimum period of time a probate estate must be open is five months. That does not mean the heirs must wait five months. The estate "personal representative can make distribution earlier than the closing if she/he is sure the property is not needed to pay claims. Probate can take much longer if there are difficult assets to deal with, such as property that does not sell. Disputes can also lengthen the time to administer the estate.   What happens in Probate? The basic steps of probate are:

- Initial Petition
- Have Will "admitted to Probate" (Testate proceedings)
- Open "Intestate" (no Will) estate
- Appoint Personal Representative (PR)
- Notice to creditors to present claims
- Determine to accept or contest claims
- Present Inventory to court and pay Inventory fee
- Pay bills, claims, expenses, taxes
- Accounting (Optional)
- Distribute estate to beneficiaries.
- Close estate.

Recommendation: For most people avoiding probate is a good idea. But, it must be done in an informed way, otherwise confusion or conflict will force expensive probate proceedings. Advice and assistance from an attorney, even if only to review one's plan, is strongly recommended.

NOTES

HOW TO AVOID PROBATE BATTLES

The best way to avoid probate battles is to see a lawyer experienced in estate planning who knows "what could possibly go wrong?" It surprises many people but parents often cause post-death court battles by children. Here are some things to consider about avoiding conflicts after you are gone.

- Have a recent Will. Circumstances change and so do intentions. Things may have changed since your old Will: A child who had an addiction when a young adult may have long recovered; A child may have borrowed thousands of dollars and never paid back anything- should that be deducted?
- Be careful about making unequal distribution. If you decide to do so, consider explaining it to the other children now rather than leaving it to them to fight it out in court.
- Make sure all beneficiary designations coordinate with the Will
- Avoid joint ownership of accounts with a child, especially a caregiver
- Carefully consider how you wish to reward a caregiver. If you do it now, you may be considered to be divesting assets for Medicaid or making an advance on inheritance.
- State your intentions regarding unpaid loans. Should they be forgiven or deducted from a child's share?
- If a child predeceases should that share lapse? Be given to his/her spouse? Be given to those grandchildren?
- Avoid homemade Wills, too often they are confusing.
- Recognize. conflicts between your children. If they do not get along now, they won't get along after death either.
- Don't try to make children get along by making them joint owners on property or joint personal representatives of your Will.
- Use a personal property memorandum – insignificant items can mean a lot to one child ("Mom would open up that old cookie jar, pull out a cookie for me and everything would be better.")
- Use extra caution after diagnosis of dementia or other cognitive impairment. See a lawyer. A Will requires enough mental capacity to know what property a person has and who he/she wants to get it after death.

NOTES

TAKE ACTION: NOW!

I said in the introduction I would urge you to take action. I think you can see that serious harm can come your way, both to your independence and how you will be remembered. Do you want to die penniless? Do you want to leave your children locked in bitter probate battles after you die? These things do happen to good people and they do not have to happen to you. You can make it through long term care "Your Way." You can save money and you can be remembered as provident parent and role model. Make an appointment to consult with an elder law attorney now.

HOW TO SELECT AN ELDER LAW ATTORNEY

I think you can see after reviewing the subjects in this booklet that having an attorney who knows elder law matters is the attorney who can give you what you need – your independence and control and ultimately your peace of mind.

How do you find an elder law attorney? Here are the best sources:
> Member of the State Bar Elder Law Section
> Member of the National Academy of Elder Law Attorneys (NAELA.ORG)
> National Elder Law Foundation (NELF.ORG) lists all Certified Elder Law Attorneys by state.
> The attorney should have a working relationship with the Alzheimer's Association, Parkinson's Foundation, ALS society, etc.
> The attorney must stay current on Elder Law and Dementia Issues and have attended regular educational programs by NAELA or the state bar.

Finally the attorney you choose must be someone you feel comfortable with. He or she must listen to you and understand your values, concerns and needs. In short you want someone who "knows what you are talking about" and can tell you the solution to your issues.

Conclusion

I hope I have completed my mission. I truly hope you found this information helpful. Just give me a call if you would like more information or to make an appointment. Our number is *(248) 356-3500.*

And, don't forget to visit our website: www.JimSchuster.com You will find many information packed articles waiting for you!

Wishing you all the best,

Jim Schuster

Certified Elder Law Attorney

www.ingramcontent.com/pod-product-compliance
Lightning Source LLC
Chambersburg PA
CBHW080939040426
42443CB00015B/3473